CW01498607

JOB SEARCH TO

JOB SECURED

A step-by-step guide for women who want to move to a

more rewarding and fulfilling career in 90 days or less

Simi Awokoya

TABLE OF CONTENTS

WHY THIS BOOK EXISTS

Before you dive into these pages, I want to share my "why" with you. This book exists because I believe every woman deserves to have a career she loves. It exists because I've seen too many women—especially Black women—settle for careers that don't serve them. They stay stuck in career fields that don't make them feel valued or honour their worth. It exists because I believe there's another way, a way that leads to work that you love, work that supports your life, and work that helps you thrive.

As a career coach, I've had the privilege of working with amazing women who all came to me for advice because they were ready to make a change. But what I've learned is that most of them did not know where to start or how to take the first step toward the career they dreamed of. They were overwhelmed by the job search process, unsure of how to present themselves, or nervous about leaping into something new. I could relate. I've been there.

I know what it's like to feel stuck. I know the frustration of wanting more—more money, more recognition, more balance—but not knowing how to get it. I know what it feels like to look around at your career and wonder, "*Is this really all there is for me?*" I've been through the anxiety of job searching, the self-doubt that comes with applying for roles you think you might not be qualified for, and the discouragement when things don't go as planned.

But what I also know is that you *don't have to settle.*

I wrote this book because I want to show you that it's possible to go from job searching to securing a new job, without all the stress, confusion, and overwhelm that typically comes with it. I want to give you the roadmap that will help you land a career you love, a career that pays you what you're worth, aligns with your values, and suits your life.

I never want another woman to feel like she has to stay in a job that doesn't light her up. Too many women in corporate feel like they're stuck—trapped in toxic work environments, underpaid, and undervalued. But the truth is, there are amazing opportunities out there for you. You just need the tools to unlock them. That's where this book comes in.

This book is a reflection of my mission to help women—especially Black women—navigate the challenges of the job market and secure the careers they deserve. I've spent years working with women from all backgrounds, and I've seen the power of their transformation when they finally take control of their careers. Whether it's doubling their salary, moving into a more senior role, or finally finding a job that aligns with their values, I've witnessed women step into their power and take bold action to change their careers for the better.

I want this book to be a turning point for you. To help you stop feeling stuck and start taking the necessary steps that will lead you to a job you're excited about. A job that gives you the salary, flexibility, and sense of fulfilment you've been craving. This book is for you if you've ever felt like you were meant for more, but didn't know how to get there. If you've ever dreamed of a job that helps you grow, supports you, and gives you the financial freedom to live the life you want, then this is for you.

I'm writing this book to show you that it's possible. I've helped countless women navigate the job search process and land roles that align with their passions, their financial goals, and their need for balance. You can do it too. You don't need another degree or years of extra experience. You don't need to apply to hundreds of jobs or wait years for a promotion. You can move forward—faster than you think—and start getting job offers that excite you.

This book exists because I want you to know that you are worthy of the career you dream about. I want you to know that the job you want is out there, and with the right tools, you can secure it. No more settling. No more burnout. No more feeling undervalued. This is your time to take control, make a move, and go from job searching to job secured.

To my incredible clients who have trusted me with their career journeys, this book is for you. And to every woman out there who is dreaming of more, who is striving for better, and who is ready to take bold steps toward the career she deserves—this book is for you, too.

May this book serve as a reminder that you are worthy of everything you desire in your career and life. May it empower you to take that next step, to trust yourself, and to secure the career you love. This is just the beginning. Let's make it happen.

CHAPTER 1:

YOU CAN LAND A NEW JOB YOU LOVE

So, you want to get a new job. You've been thinking about moving for a while, but the whole process makes you anxious. You don't know where to start, or maybe you have already started exploring your options, applying for jobs and even interviewing but no luck so far.

If you relate to the above, I totally understand where you are coming from. I receive several messages per week from working professionals who are in the same shoes as you. Messages like this:

"Hi Simi,

Hope you're well, and lovely to e-meet you!

I'm currently looking to change job roles and wanted to find out what coaching services you offer for candidates looking to change jobs/currently applying for new roles. I want to make sure I'm maximising my efforts effectively when it comes to my job applications and make sure I'm utilising all the necessary skills to find my next role.

If you're able to get back to me soon on your services that would be great! I look forward to hearing back from you."

The client I received this message from had been with her employer for a couple of years and had been promoted but had not received a salary increase. She was looking for a higher-paying job at a company with a more friendly working culture. After our initial conversation, it was clear that she was motivated to get a new job. However, she shared that she found the whole job search process intimidating. Despite the promotion she had received at her current job, she felt her experience and skills were not enough to get the new job she wanted.

My client and I worked together and in less than 90 days, she had received and signed a new job offer. This new job gave her:

- A significant salary increase paying her £20k more than her previous role
- The opportunity to work in a new industry that aligned with her interests
- Better work-life balance and the ability to work remotely more frequently

- A more diverse company with friendly colleagues where she felt a sense of belonging

She went from spending years at a company where she felt stagnant and stressed to getting a new job where she could make more money and feel fulfilled without having to gain more experience or additional qualifications.

Can you imagine how incredible it would be for you to experience the same for your career? I definitely can!

Imagine This:

- What if you could secure a **higher-paying job** with a **more senior job title** that finally reflects your experience?
- What if you could **wake up every morning feeling fulfilled** because you have **a career that allows you to make an impact** in a way that feels important to you?
- What if you could **work for a company where you felt prioritised, valued and recognised for your contributions**?

- What if you could have a career that gives you the flexibility to balance your day job, personal projects and family life?

The times I have moved to a new job have been the most significant and positive career changes I have ever made.

After 5 years with my first employer after university, I decided I was tired of feeling undervalued and underappreciated. On paper, it looked like I had my dream job but in reality, I was overwhelmed and unmotivated.

When I changed jobs, I realised what true career fulfilment was! My new job helped me to double my salary and gave me a company car, a sign-on bonus and company stocks. I finally felt compensated in a way that felt aligned with me.

This new job meant I was able to decide when and where I was able to work. I could work from home any time I liked! This was even before the 2020 pandemic. My new employer allowed employees to work where suited them best.

My new job also invested in me. I was able to have a yearly allowance to spend on new qualifications or invest in my health and wellness.

Most importantly, my new job allowed me to live my life on my own terms. In my previous jobs, I always wondered what it would be like to have a family and kids because there was little to no work-life balance. While at my new job, I got married and had 2 kids. I was able to take a year off for each maternity leave (with full pay), still get promotions and grow my career.

Moving to a new job gave me opportunities in my career that I didn't know were possible. Just by making a career change, I received more money, more freedom and more rewards.

Does this sound like you?

- You want to have a higher salary
- You want to move to another company or industry
- You want to meet your financial goals so you can save, spend and invest

- You want a more senior position
- You want to spend more time with your kids during the week
- You want to move to a company that promotes a good work-life blend and healthy boundaries

If any of those points struck a chord, you are probably in a job that you are not happy in, and it is currently not meeting your needs. You might have tried to look for another job, but you might have received disappointments; application/
interview rejections or job offers that do not meet your expectations.

I wrote this book to help you use your existing work experience and transferable skills to attract the jobs you want, give you a peaceful job search and help you make an empowered career move.

You can navigate your job search and secure a more fulfilling job without the stress:

- Without doing another degree

- Without applying for hundreds of jobs
- Without waiting forever for a promotion
- Without feeling guilty for not spending time with your family
- Without tolerating a toxic work environment
- Without being burnt out or bored

However, moving jobs seems stressful when you have questions about how to navigate your job search:

- How do you know what jobs and industries to apply to?
- How do you know which jobs will pay you well?
- How do you know which jobs will give you the flexibility you want?
- How do you present your experience well when applying for jobs?
- How do you make your experience relevant when changing industries?
- How do you navigate the interview stage if it's a job you have never done before?

- How do you make sure you get a good job offer and don't end up in the wrong career?
- How do you resign from your job and get ready for your new job?

All these questions are probably in your head right now and it can be very confusing when you don't have all the answers yet.

I've got you all covered.

The great thing going for you is that you can secure a new job that you love, even if you have never moved jobs before.

Even if you have moved jobs before and it didn't turn out for the best.

This can be all made easy by using my **Search To Secured Method.**

The method is the proven job search process used by my clients who have secured new jobs that are higher paying and more fulfilling across multiple industries, levels of seniority and in different parts of the world.

Hi! I'm Simi, a career coach for women in corporate.

I'm an award-winning career coach with over a decade of experience running programs and career workshops for women in corporate.

I've helped 100s of women move to new jobs that significantly increased their salary and finally helped them secure a fulfilling career.

Before working with me: *They were confused about the steps to take in their career, they were burnt out from applying to hundreds of jobs, and they were worried about navigating the hiring process.*

And I knew I couldn't sit back and watch women in corporate struggle anymore.

Instead, I wanted to create an easy, straightforward way for women in corporate to secure a more rewarding and flexible career without confusion, trial and error or getting overwhelmed with the job market.

That's how my signature **Search To Secured Method** was created to help more women go from job searching to securing their highest-paid and most fulfilling jobs yet!

I'll show you exactly what you need to quickly understand the job market and collapse the time it takes for you to get a new job you love.

By the end of this book, you will learn:

- How to start your job search and successfully secure a new job in 90 days or less
- How to find the right jobs, companies and industries that suit your life and your career goals
- The biggest mistake most working professionals make when looking for a new job (and how to avoid it)
- How to identify which jobs to apply to and how to ensure the applications lead to interviews
- Job search secrets to help you build rapport with recruiters and hiring managers so they consider you as the best candidate

- How to navigate the interview process, spot red flags and green flags and get a job offer from the company you want
- How to get the best job offer for the next phase of your career and how to successfully negotiate so that your new job pays you well, is flexible for your needs and leads to a fulfilling career
- How to resign from your old job gracefully and start your new career with confidence

I know you can get a new job you love. You just need some guidance from someone who knows how to help you make it a reality.

That's why you got this book. I am here to give you the step-by-step process through every chapter until you get to the very last page.

Ready to secure the job you love?

I can't wait to show you how!

CHAPTER 2:

THE JOB MARKET CAN BE CONFUSING (WHEN YOU DON'T KNOW WHAT YOU ARE LOOKING FOR)

Whenever my clients tell me that they have been confused about where to start when it comes to moving to a new job, **I can completely relate because I have been there.**

In hindsight, I started a career I had no business being in and needed to move jobs but I didn't know what job to do next and I also had a deep-rooted fear of making the wrong move.

This is what my career used to look like:

- I worked round the clock and my manager would message me to log in on the weekends.
- My promotions only got me a 3% raise which didn't make a difference to my bank account.
- I worked at a large global organisation yet I was earning less than £50k a year.
- My department had a toxic work environment, I was not able to work from home and I didn't know if I would be able to start a family or have kids with the pressure I had from work.

- Living on a not-so-great salary in central London was tough and I did not have a "bank of mum and dad" to rescue me.
- I was paying rent, had 5 figures in student loans, had loads of expenses and was living paycheck to paycheck.

I knew I could not stay this way moving forward.

However, I had some thoughts that made me feel like moving jobs was an unrealistic fantasy and I should just stay where I am.

Thoughts like:

"You can't build wealth with a 9 to 5"

"It's impossible to have a thriving career while being a mum or present for your family"

"Having a stressful job is part of the territory of working in corporate"

"I guess it's normal to be the only Black person or woman in the department"

Until I realised it didn't have to stay that way.

I could rewrite my career story.

I went from earning under £50k a year to doubling my salary in a few weeks and went on to:

- Increase my salary by £10k-£50k multiple times when moving jobs
- Pay off all my student loans
- Get on the property ladder
- Become a landlord
- Build a 5-figure investment portfolio
- Get a fully paid 12-month maternity leave with a £75k bonus
- Build a career I love and be a present mum and wife at the same time

This all happened because I learnt how to use my skills and experience to move to a higher-paying and more fulfilling career, and most importantly, **I figured out what I wanted out of the new job.**

Many people say they want to move jobs but they don't prioritise what they want out of the new job. When you don't have priorities, you become confused.

And that's why I wrote this book, to help you get unstuck and help you take the right next steps in securing a new job you love:

- To show you that you don't need to play the waiting game to increase your salary and have a fulfilling career.
- To show you that changing careers is not a 5-year plan, it's a plan for NOW that can be stress-free and straightforward.
- To show you the myths and misconceptions surrounding moving to a new job are not true.

As you go through this book, I will show you how to figure out what you are looking for so:

- You will be able to increase your salary without getting more experience

- You will be confident in applying and interviewing for roles you haven't done before
- You will be able to secure a higher-paying and more fulfilling job even during recessions and layoffs
- You will know how to identify roles and companies that have the budget to pay you what you want
- You will not have to wait to see how things go. You will be in control and in a career that helps you become well-paid and fulfilled

I can't wait to guide you through the process!

CHAPTER 3:

YOUR SOLUTION: THE SEARCH TO SECURED METHOD

When you first started this book, I mentioned that I received dozens of messages from working professional women sharing their job search concerns and struggles with me. Many of them worked with me as their coach, and I introduced them to the **Search To Secured Method** to help them secure a new job.

The Search To Secured Method is my proven roadmap to help working professional women use their existing skills and experience during their job search to secure a higher-paying and more fulfilling job in 90 days or less.

So, why did I create this method?

After moving jobs several times myself, I realised that navigating a job search is not a process of trial and error. It's a process of certainty. However, so many women are told to see how it goes when they are looking for a new opportunity. This is far from reality.

So, I took it upon myself to design a step-by-step process to help working professionals navigate the job search process regardless of the type of new job they wanted.

Most people want a new job that helps them change 1 or more of these things in their career:

1. Level:

    You might want to move to a more senior, management or leadership position.

2. Industry:

    You might want to move to a new sector, field or subject matter.

3. Culture:

    You might want to move to a company that shares your values, has better flexibility and improves well-being or is in a new country/location.

Not sure what kind of career change you want? Watch this mini-training which helps you identify what type of career change suits you best and how to achieve it.

https://youtu.be/GKRynamGRQU

To change level, you may have considered waiting to get more years of experience.

To change industry, you may have considered getting another degree or qualification.

To change your company culture, you may have considered just staying where you are out of the fear that you won't be able to find better.

This is exactly where the Search To Secured Method comes in. You don't need more experience, another degree/certification, or to "see how it goes". You just need a 4-phase approach.

The 4 Phases of the Search To Secured Method

Phase 1: Job Search Goals

Phase 2: Applications

Phase 3: Interviews

Phase 4: Job Offers & Negotiation

Here's a breakdown of each phase:

Phase 1: Job Search Goals

The goal of this phase is to identify jobs that align with your skills at companies that can pay you what you want. Most people think their job search starts with applying for jobs. NEWSFLASH: It does not. It starts with figuring out how you want to position yourself in the job market so you can secure the job you want. This is important so you do not waste time exploring job opportunities that are not the right fit for you.

During this phase, you will:

1. Decide on the high-paying jobs you want that matches your skill set without having to get another degree or certification.

    -This applies specifically to people who want to get a more senior role or want to change industries.

2. Identify companies that pay you what you want and fit your work-life balance.

    -This will help you ensure you get a new employer that values you and also has a good working environment and culture.

3. Define your salary expectations so you know what jobs are worth your time.

    -It is so crucial to know this upfront so you can filter out jobs that do not pay well and save you from being disappointed down the line.

Phase 2: Applications

The goal of this phase is to use your skills and work experience to apply to and attract the jobs you want. Simply put: you need to learn how to look good on paper a.k.a apply to jobs that convert into an interview.

Applying is the 2nd phase of the job search once you have identified your goals because now you have direction. When you have figured out what types of jobs will serve you best, now is the time to become attractive for those jobs and apply for them.

The best part of this is when this phase is done right, jobs will apply to you too. This means that people who are hiring will reach out to you to share job opportunities that are a good fit without you applying.

During this phase, you will:

1. Create your CV/Resume (depending on where you live in the world you might call it a CV or a resume) that makes your work experience relevant to the jobs you apply for.

2. Create your Cover letter to pitch yourself to hiring managers and show your skills and experience as a solution to the company's current problems.

3. Optimise your LinkedIn profile so you can become attractive to recruiters and receive leads on new job opportunities that align with your goals.

Phase 3: Interviews

The goal of this phase is to learn how to highlight your skills and work experience so you can secure the job. This phase is about knowing how to show up well during the interview stage so you can convert the interview into a job offer. You need to be able to tell a compelling story about your career that positions you as the top candidate for the job you want.

During this phase, you will navigate the 3 phases of the interview process:

1. Before the interview

   Articulate your experience during the recruiter discussion and check if the job is aligned with your expectations.

2. The interview

   Show up at the interview as the top candidate by highlighting your relevant experience and competencies for the job.

3. After the interview

   Ask the right questions and close the interview by leaving a good impression so you can secure the job offer.

Phase 4: Job Offers & Negotiation

The goal of this phase is to select the right job offer by negotiating so you can maximise your total compensation and benefits at your new job. This phase is often missed by working professionals when they get a job offer.

Moving to a new job is a straightforward way to increase your salary and maximise your total compensation and benefits. However, companies will rarely make their best offer upfront. You have to negotiate to get the best offer. Failure to negotiate could result in your colleagues earning more than you or having to start another job search sooner than expected because you feel underpaid at that job.

During this phase, you will learn how to make a fully informed decision when selecting your job offer:

1. Selecting the offer

    Understand your overall compensation for the job and what parts of the offer can be negotiated.

2. Accepting the offer

    Learn the psychology behind a job offer conversation with a recruiter and the Do's & Don'ts when accepting a job offer.

3. Negotiating the offer

    A walkthrough of what to prepare for when negotiating your job offer.

These 4 phases of the Search To Secured Method have helped hundreds of my coaching clients secure higher-paying and more fulfilling jobs in 90 days or less.

Check out success stories from women who have used the Search To Secured Method to navigate their job search and move to new jobs:

https://coach-simi.com/client-results

Now it's time to take action through the next chapters of the book where I will walk you through the Search To Secured Method step-by-step.

CHAPTER 4:

BEFORE YOU START YOUR JOB SEARCH, DO THIS

Before we dive into the 4 phases of the Search To Secured method, I need to set some expectations with you so you can see results in your job search and avoid the trap of feeling stuck and confused when it comes to getting a new role.

Step 1: Create a blank slate and treat this as a new beginning

You probably bought this book because you are tired of the way your job search has been going or you are worried about getting started with your job search. The Search To Secured Method is designed to change your perspective on how to navigate the job market and land a new job. You will discover that you might end up doing things you've never thought you would do such as: asking for the salary budget upfront, rejecting interviews/job offers or putting yourself first in a way you haven't before. This is all part of the journey and you might find this to be a huge mindset shift for you but it will be all worth it in the end.

To see results you haven't seen before, you have to do things differently.

Trust the process just like my clients have and you will land a new job in no time.

Step 2: Cultivate an abundance mindset

Now is the time to get rid of negative thoughts like *"the job market is saturated"* or *"the job market is bad"*. These thoughts are not true.

I have worked with clients to secure new jobs during difficult seasons like the 2020 pandemic and 2022 economic downturn.

Companies are still hiring regardless of what the economy is saying and there are more than enough opportunities to go around. As a career coach, I see so many women settle into jobs they are not happy with out of fear and also accept new job positions that they know are not a right fit for them.

This book is designed to give you a clear strategy to ensure you are making career decisions out of empowerment and not fear.

The right job for you is out there! Approach your job search from a place of abundance (not scarcity).

Step 3: Time block and give yourself milestones

There's a popular saying that goes, "Fail to plan, plan to fail". Navigating your job search requires a plan and that is exactly what this book is going to give you.

You might have spent months or years trying to move jobs without being sure of the timeline. In this book, we are going to give you a 90-day action plan to help you strategically explore the job market and secure a new job.

Each phase of the Search To Secured method is time-blocked to give you a chance to allocate the right amount of time to it. Please do not rush through it or overthink it.

Search To Secured Method 90-day Timeline

Phase 1: Job Search Goals (Day 1-10) => Timeblock 10 days

Phase 2: Applications (Day 11-50) => Timeblock 40 days (1 month+)

Phase 3: Interviews (Day 51-80) => Timeblock 30 days (1 month)

Phase 4: Job Offers & Negotiation (Day 81-90)

=>Timeblock 10 days

Many of my clients follow the step-by-step process and see results. You will be no different.

TAKE ACTION

Download your 90-day job search planner.

This planner ensures you have completed all the milestones of each phase of the Search To Secured method. You will walk away with a breakdown of all the tasks you need to complete from this book in a more condensed form for you to print or keep handy on your laptop or phone.

Visit https://coach-simi.com/planner to download the 90-day job search planner.

CHAPTER 5:

JOB SEARCH GOALS

Mindset Shift: Start How You Mean To Continue

When starting your job search, it is important to set your intentions early on in the process so you do not become distracted or confused about the type of job opportunities you're looking for.

In this chapter, you are going to learn how to identify jobs that align with your skills at companies that can pay you what you want.

Find Your Job Search Focus

To avoid an endless job search, you need to have a focus for your job search. By "focus", I mean knowing the type of jobs you want and having clarity on where you are going and where your destination is. I recommend having a focus so you're not confused or distracted while you are on your job search, applying, interviewing or accepting the job offer.

THERE ARE 4 AREAS YOU CAN FOCUS ON

	SAME INDUSTRY	DIFFERENT INDUSTRY
SAME JOB	Same Job Same Industry	Same Job Different Industry
DIFFERENT JOB	Different Job Same Industry	Different Job Different Industry

There are 4 areas you can focus on in your job search. You can focus on a combination of jobs and industries:

1. Same job, Same industry

Moving to a job title similar to what you have now.

2. Same job, Different industry

Moving to a similar job title but operating in a different context/sector.

3. Different job, Same industry

Moving to a different job title in a context/sector similar to the one you are in now.

4. Different job, Different industry

Moving to a completely new job title in a different sector. This is called a career pivot.

A practical example:

If you are a Product Manager (PM) at a financial institution looking for a new job this would look like:

1. Same job, Same industry

Moving to another PM position at a financial institution.

2. Same job, Different industry

Moving to another PM position at an advertising agency.

3. Different job, Same industry

Moving to a Sales Executive position at a financial institution.

4. Different job, Different industry

Moving to a Sales Executive position at an advertising agency.

In summary, your job search focus can be in 4 areas.

However, when you want to be well-positioned in the job market and be intentional about your job search, **you should focus on 1 or 2 of these areas for your job search focus. So out of those 4 options, you should prioritise 2 at most.**

If you have more than two areas of focus, it means you really haven't decided what you want out of the next stage of your career. This will lead to overwhelm during your job search or, even worse, regrets about the new job that you get.

So, how do you decide on the 1 or 2 areas that you want to focus on?

CRITERIA YOU CAN USE TO DECIDE THE 1-2 AREAS TO FOCUS YOUR JOB SEARCH

	SAME INDUSTRY	DIFFERENT INDUSTRY
SAME JOB	Previous role success	Proven industry interest, Previous role success
DIFFERENT JOB	Transferable skills, Proven role interest with previous responsibilities	Transferable skills, Industry interest, Passion to learn

Here is the criteria and questions you can ask yourself to help you prioritise the selection of your 1-2 job search focus area(s):

1. Same job, Same industry

Previous role success: Have you done the job before and did you enjoy it?

2.   Same job, Different industry

Proven industry interest & Previous role success: Can you show that you can use your skills and experience from previous jobs in a different context/sector?

3.   Different job, Same industry

Transferable skills, Proven role interest with previous responsibilities: Can you show that you have relevant skills from your previous jobs that will help you be successful in a different job title in the same context/sector?

4.   Different job, Different industry

Transferable skills, Industry interest, Passion to learn: Can you show that you have learnt relevant skills to the new industry you want to work in and that you have a vested interest in learning and growing in this new job and industry?

Based on these different criteria, you can pick the 1-2 that you can confidently speak to that will help you narrow down your job search focus and ensure you navigate the rest of your job search with intention.

Understand Job Descriptions

Now that you know what your job search focus is, you need to validate that it is correct and aligned with what you want for your career moving forward.

The easiest way to check this is by understanding the job descriptions for the job you want.

So many people get intimidated by job descriptions and feel they are not qualified for jobs even when it's the job they want. If you fit the criteria for the job search focus, there is nothing to fear. I'm going to show you how to quickly assess a job description using 3 pillars to ensure it aligns with your job search focus.

Pillar 1: Qualifications

You do not need to be overqualified. Aim to meet 60%! Your transferable skills can cover the rest when you meet the job search focus criteria.

Pillar 2: Responsibilities

Look for skills used in the job descriptions for jobs you want. These skills will be needed for the application phase of your job search.

Pillar 3: Preferences

Pay attention to the language used to describe the nature of the responsibilities. Some descriptions give away if the job is low paying or a toxic work environment.

Use these 3 pillars in combination with your 1-2 job search focus areas to ensure that the jobs and industries you are interested in are in line with your goals. This process will give you immense clarity before you even start applying for jobs.

Identify Companies

Now that you have validated your 1-2 job search focus areas regarding jobs and industries, it's time to figure out which companies are the right fit for you.

Your aim should be to move to a company that pays you what you want and fits your work-life balance because ideally, your next job should be higher paying and more fulfilling than the one you have now/your previous job.

We need the company to pay you more AND be more fulfilling than your most recent job! We need it to be both.

If it's just higher paying and not fulfilling, then you'll be getting paid well, but you will not be happy in your career, and you'll probably have no time outside of work to enjoy the money you are making.

If it's fulfilling but doesn't pay well, you will be happy, but you will feel undervalued for the work you do and you definitely don't want that!

You want to work at a good company that pays you very well and lets you have a fulfilling life both inside and outside work.

But what is a "good company" anyway?

"Good company" is subjective. "Good company" looks different for everyone. Some people want to work for companies that are really fast-paced, always making changes, and have a start-up-type culture.

Whereas some people love stability. They want minimal change. They want a company that pretty much has been doing things the same way they've been doing things for years.

So "good" looks different for everyone. A good company to you in the present day may look completely different to what you thought was good several years ago. You've probably changed, have different desires and have different goals for your life. It's really important at this stage of your job search to reassess what a good company looks like for you.

You have to set new standards for what a good employer is for you moving forward, and I usually teach my clients to categorise their standards into these 3 categories:

1. **Standard #1: Money=> Identifying if the company pays well**

Some questions you should ask yourself to determine if the company pays well are:

- Is the job in the front office helping the business make money?
- Is the job a crucial support function in the company?
- Is the job attracting new clients?
- Is the company close to a city or cosmopolitan area where the cost of living is higher?

If you can answer "yes" to most of these questions, the company may reach your Money standard.

2. **Standard #2: Freedom=> Identifying if the company fits your lifestyle**

Some questions you should ask yourself to determine if the company will fit your lifestyle:

- Can you work from home?
- Can you work from anywhere/remotely?

- How many holiday days do you have?
- Do you want a 4-day work week/to work part-time?

The more flexible the answers to these questions are, the more likely you will have a good work-life balance at the company and it may reach your Freedom standard.

3. **Standard #3: Rewards=> Identifying if the company has perks and benefits**

Some questions you should ask yourself to determine if the company rewards employees outside of salary/regular pay cheque:

- Does the company pay a commission or a quarterly/yearly bonus?
- Would you receive stocks as part of compensation?
- Do you get a private healthcare and pension plan? And does it kick in from day 1?

If you can answer "yes" to most of these questions, the company may reach your Rewards standard.

Define Your Salary Expectations

To have an intentional job search that leads to a job worth your time, it's a great idea to define your salary expectations before you even get started.

The whole point of getting a new job is to get something better than what you currently have. There is no point even considering jobs that cannot pay you what you want.

One of the main reasons why many women don't feel fulfilled with their careers is because they don't feel well compensated. Unfortunately, many of them are afraid to walk away from these careers because they feel they can't get another job that will pay them more.

That's why I encourage my clients following the Search To Secured method to always start by having **a walkaway number.**

Your walkaway number is the minimum salary you will be willing to accept for your next job. If the salary offered by the company is less than your walkaway number, then you simply walk away from the job opportunity.

How to define your walkaway number

Your walkaway number should be a significant increase on your current salary. This is at least 5 figures a.k.a £10k (£10,000) and above.

It should be a number that will make a tangible difference to your monthly take-home pay.

I usually recommend your walkaway number should be £10k to £50k higher than what you currently earn. This is a proven range for a salary increase. You can check out some of my client success stories here showing that this type of salary increase is very achievable. https://coach-simi.com/client-results

To see how this impacts your take-home pay, you can search online for a salary calculator website that shows you what your monthly earnings can be based on your walkaway number.

Conduct salary research

After brainstorming your potential walkaway number, it is time to validate your salary expectations by researching salaries for the jobs and industries you are interested in.

There are 2 ways you can do this: via external data and via networking.

YOUR SALARY EXPECTATIONS: CONDUCTING RESEARCH

VIA EXTERNAL DATA	VIA NETWORKING
PAY TRANSPARENCY WEBSITES: Glassdoor Payscale Levels.fyi	**ASK PEOPLE IN THE JOB/AT THE COMPANY** "What salary range should a person in <JOB TITLE> expect to receive?"
PAY TRANSPARENCY FORUMS: Fishbowl Blind	**ASK RECRUITER** "What is the budget for this role?"

Via external data

When conducting research via external data, you can use pay transparency websites and forums such as:

https://www.glassdoor.com/

https://www.payscale.com/

https://www.levels.fyi/

https://www.fishbowlapp.com/

https://www.teamblind.com/salary

These websites allow you to filter by job title and company to see what other people have anonymously shared about their salary. Remember, this is just a subset of employees who have chosen to share.

Salary research using external data shows you how much you could potentially earn in a job at a company. However, the data does not tell you if the employee who shared their salary is performing or underperforming. This means you should never use external data alone for validating your salary expectations as you could unintentionally lowball yourself.

For example, if you go on Glassdoor.com and you see that a job at a certain company is paying £70k, then you get to the interview and say your salary expectation is £70k, you could end up making a big mistake. You could find out later down the line that the budget for the role was £90k and you would've missed out on a £20k salary increase because you relied on Glassdoor alone.

For this reason, you must always combine research using external data with a form of research via networking.

<u>Via networking</u>

- When conducting research via networking, you can ask people who currently have the job title you're interested in/work in a company you're interested in:

Ask: "What salary range should a person in <insert job title> expect to receive?"

This way you're asking them what your expectations should be without asking them for their specific salary (some people might be uncomfortable sharing). You're able to get an insight based on their time in the role. Combined with the number of years of experience they have, you should be able to get a pulse on if your walkaway number is in the right range.

- When conducting research via networking, you can ask the recruiter directly for the budget for the role.

Ask: "What is the budget for this role?"

This is the best way to find out what specific jobs and industries are willing to pay. Knowing this gives you a lot of leverage because you can then know whether it's the right job for you based on your salary expectations (walkaway number) or what others who have been in the role have mentioned you should expect.

NOTE #1: Before attending a job interview, please ask for the budget or share your salary expectations with the recruiter to avoid wasting time.

NOTE #2: Do not share your current salary with company recruiters. Women are often caught in this trap of sharing what they currently earn, limiting their earning potential. You don't need to share what you currently earn. It's not relevant, and it doesn't dictate or say anything about you. Share your salary expectations (walkaway number) instead.

Job Search Goals: Your Action Plan

You have learnt about the 4 steps in establishing your job search goals:

1. Find Your Job Search Focus

2. Understand Job Descriptions

3. Identify Companies

4. Define Your Salary Expectations

Here's your action plan for the first 10 days of your job search (Day 1-10):

- Write down the job titles and industries you are considering moving to.
- Categorise them into the 4 possible job search focus areas:

    1. Same job, Same industry

    2. Same job, Different industry

    3. Different job, Same industry

    4. Different job, Different industry

- Prioritise your top 2 job search focus areas (based on the criteria shared in this chapter).

- Search online for job descriptions for your top 2 job search focus areas and validate if you are interested in them based on the 3 job description pillars (Qualifications, Responsibilities & Preferences).

- Search online for companies in your industry of choice and validate if the jobs and companies can meet your standards of a good company (Money, Freedom & Rewards).

- Define your salary expectations (ideally your walkaway number should be £10k to £50k higher than your current salary).

- Validate your salary expectations using external data and networking with professionals in the job and recruiters.

CHAPTER 6:

APPLICATIONS

Mindset Shift: Always choose quality over quantity

When you have decided on your job search goals, you are now in a good place to start applying for jobs.

In this chapter, you are going to learn how to turn your job applications into interviews using your CV/resume, Cover Letter and LinkedIn profile. You will learn how to create high-quality applications that lead to results for your job search and not just apply to as many jobs as possible (a.k.a treating it like a numbers game).

5 Applications Secret

For decades, people have told professionals looking for a new job to "apply to as many jobs as possible". This is not optimal advice because it encourages you to apply to any job you come across, which leads you to submit very generic applications that result in your application not being seen by the recruiter or, even worse, rejected.

The 5 Applications Secret is a concept I created to show you that applications are about "Quality over quantity". I am confident that when you learn how to apply to jobs correctly, you will start getting invited to interviews by submitting only 5 applications (or less).

So where did the "apply to as many jobs as possible" advice originate from?

In the working world, we are often told to prioritise busyness over productivity. So, in a job search, it's very common to hear that someone has been applying to jobs for months on end and still hasn't been invited to an interview.

This often happens because they have not completed Phase 1 of the Search To Secured method. In other words, they have no job search goals. This means they have no clarity on the type of job titles they want, the industry type or the salary they want. They are just applying and seeing what sticks. This often results in the hiring manager and the recruiter looking at their application, thinking it's generic, so they'll either ignore it or reject the application.

I like to recommend a different approach: The 5 Applications Secret.

Start by giving yourself this challenge at the beginning of your job search:

I want to apply for 5 jobs that are highly relevant to the skills and experience that I want to use in my next job.

By doing this, you get crystal clear and intentional about how you present yourself in your applications.

You may eventually apply for more than 5 jobs but giving yourself this challenge at the beginning of your job search makes you very selective and specific about the jobs you apply for. Which in turn, results in you creating more impactful applications that give you results (invitations to interview).

Create Your CV

As a working professional, you've had a CV (or resume) at some point in your career. Either to get a job or to put yourself forward for a promotion or opportunity.

Unfortunately, most people think that their CV is just a list of their work experience that is updated as the years go on.

However, when it comes to applying for a new job, your CV is not just a list.

Your CV should be tailored for every application you submit. You should not be using the same CV to apply for all the jobs you want.

Your CV should be specific to the job you are applying for, not the jobs you've had in the past.

The recruiter or hiring manager will be looking specifically for certain traits in candidates, so you want to make sure you have a good chance.

A habit a lot of people have is when they create a CV, they end up just writing about the jobs they've had in the past. When you've seen the job description for the job you want, you should be describing your past work experience in the context of the job you want.

You want to show that you already have the capability of excelling at the job. So, you need to apply for the job you want, not make it about your past jobs.

Think of your CV like a pitch. Think about a show like Dragon's Den or Shark Tank.

They are pitching shows where people are pitching business ideas to investors. When guests come on and pitch their products or services, they have a specific customer in mind. They talk about how their product or service can solve a specific problem.

The same goes for your CV. Your CV has to be written with a specific job in mind. You need to present your experience in a way that solves a company's problem.

Your CV is not just about you. The company should be able to look at your CV and think, "We need her in our company!"

So how do you know your CV is effective? Here are 4 signs your CV is doing what it's meant to:

1. It passes the Applicant Tracking System

Many recruitment teams use a system called Applicant Tracking System (ATS) to keep track of applications. They are also able to filter through to see the most relevant applications, especially when there are many applicants for the job. When they filter, they add intelligence to the system to look for specific keywords, words and phrases in CVs. With this in mind, you want to make sure that your CV contains skills mentioned in the job description.

You also want to ensure that it's a simple file type like a Word Doc or PDF because you want the words to be able to be picked up in the search that the ATS intelligence is looking for.

2. It grabs the recruiters' attention

You want to make sure that the job you're applying for is written on your CV. Many people put their current job title at the top of their CV which is distracting to the recruiter as that is not the job position they are hiring for. I always recommend that you put the job title you're applying for next to your name. Make sure that you start your CV with a professional summary that speaks to your experience and is relevant to the job title you are applying for.

3. It is succinct and to the point

Every word in your CV should be purposeful. 1-2 pages is ideal.

If you have 0-5 years of experience, 1 page works. If you have 5+ years, 2 pages are justified.

4. It is impact-led and specific to the job

When describing your past work experience you want to speak about your impact and not just the tasks you did. Your CV is an opportunity to quantify your achievements and highlight your transferable skills. This is specifically important if you are pivoting careers (you want a new job that you have never done before in an industry you have never been in).

So now that we know what makes a CV effective, how do we structure it?

A lot of times, when professional women write their CVs, they don't know why they are writing what they are writing. This is why I want to share with you exactly what should be in your CV and why. We're going to be very intense and intentional about what you put in your CV moving forward.

Here is how you should structure your CV:

CV STRUCTURE

- Name + Job title you are applying for
- Contact Details
- Professional Summary
- Skills
- Work Experience
- Education
- Volunteering & Awards

→ Name + Job title you are applying for

You need to include your name and the job title you are applying for in your CV. This is so crucial because you want to show the recruiter that you are specifically applying for this job. They will be looking through dozens of applications, so you really need to stand out. This will show when you specifically apply for the job. It's a highly effective way to ensure that it's tailored and they know you are applying specifically for that position.

→ Contact Details

I advise you to include your email address, a link to your LinkedIn profile, your phone number and also the city and country where you live. If you are looking to relocate for a job opportunity, be sure to include "Willing to relocate". DO NOT put your full address. So many people you do not know online will get an opportunity to see your CV and it is best not to include your residential address for your safety and security.

→ Professional Summary

Think of your professional summary as an elevator pitch. If you only had 30-45 seconds to tell someone why you are the best candidate for the job, what would you say? Your professional summary should be 3- 5 sentences of your work experience that showcases the value you can provide to a future employer hiring for the job you are applying for.

→ Skills

The skills section in your CV is vital. It shows that you are capable of doing the job you are applying for. You will find the skills required in the job description.

For example, in a marketing analyst role, some skills are marketing strategy, product marketing, marketing campaigns, project management, etc. All these things will be in the job descriptions. Therefore, ensure that you include the skills you have in your CV.

→ Work Experience

Your work experience section is a summary of the past work experiences you've had with previous employers. For each employer, I recommend using 3-5 bullet points that are achievement-based. These bullet points should not be your responsibilities. This is one of the biggest mistakes I see professionals make. Responsibilities belong in a job description, not a CV. Your work experience section should highlight your achievements in your career and showcase your potential for success in the job you are applying for.

→ Education

Include your undergraduate or postgraduate education. You may also want to include any relevant qualifications that are relevant to the job you're applying for.

→ Volunteering & Awards

Any volunteering opportunities or industry awards that position you as a good candidate should be included in your CV. This section is optional but makes you look well-rounded and a potential value-add to the hiring organisation

Your CV is the key to converting your applications into interviews. You've learnt why your application should be targeted, why you shouldn't be applying for hundreds of jobs and why it's important to create specific targeted applications for each job you apply for.

Write Your Cover Letter

Cover letters are touchy subjects for most people. Some people would rather not submit one as part of their application once they see it's optional on the application form.

I recommend you always write a cover letter for 3 main reasons.

Reason #1: A cover letter can speed up the hiring process

Cover letters can be used in various ways: in an application, to follow up on an application or to get an interview without applying.

Cover letters are not only used for the application itself but also to introduce yourself to managers and recruiters who are hiring before the formal application process starts.

If you have a cover letter written, you would be able to use the contents in an email or LinkedIn message to present yourself as an impressive candidate and potentially fast-track your hiring even before the application process officially starts.

Reason #2: A cover letter gives you more credibility

A cover letter can be used to increase your credibility as a candidate and increase your likelihood of getting an interview.

A cover letter is specifically valuable for a:

- Career pivot: you trying to change to a career path you have no direct experience in

- Career gap: you have taken several months or years out of work and want to get back into the working world

- In-demand job market: you are looking for a new job opportunity in a very popular industry/sector

Reason #3: A cover letter helps make your application more visible

As I mentioned earlier in the chapter, many recruitment teams use a system called Applicant Tracking System (ATS) to keep track of applications. When you have a Cover Letter, it's another chance to get your application prioritised by the ATS (because your cover letter has relevant skills in the job description) and increase your chances of your application being seen by the recruiter.

So now that you know the advantage of having a cover letter, let us dive into how to structure your Cover Letter:

Part 1: Your Introduction

You want to share your background and expertise and tell them how it matches the company's vision. It's really good that you set the scene to ensure that they understand why you're applying and why you're a good fit.

Part 2: Your Experience

You want to tell them why you're a good fit for the job. Give them one or two examples by fleshing out the achievement-based bullet point that you've put in your CV.

Part 3: Your Conclusion

You want to end showing value with a call to action and inviting them to reach out to you to find out more to move your application forward. You really want your cover letter to be succinct to the point and show your value immediately.

Now you have learned the importance of a cover letter, why you should never skip writing one and how to structure your cover letter.

Optimise Your LinkedIn Profile

LinkedIn is the ultimate hack when it comes to getting a new job. It's so much more than an online social media platform. It is a powerful opportunity for you to become attractive to more jobs during your job search and be visible to recruiters who are hiring.

Your LinkedIn profile is an opportunity to build your career brand so recruiters reach out to you to ask for your CV and ask you to interview for jobs without you even applying.

Here are the things you need in place to make sure your LinkedIn profile is optimised to have recruiters reaching out to you.

Profile Photo: A professional picture where your face can be seen.

Why? Makes you personable and likely to be reached out to. Change your profile photo visibility settings if it's connections and network only.

Headline: Put the main job title you want in your headline.

Why? Allows you to be approached for job opportunities you will likely want.

Recruiters can search for certain keywords using LinkedIn Recruiter. LinkedIn Recruiter is a version of LinkedIn for talent sourcing that recruiters have access to for a fee and it allows them to search for candidates based on what they do and what they've included in their keywords. That means they get to find talent faster and they get to interview candidates faster.

About Section: A professional summary.

Why? Allows people to learn about your career brand and achievements. You can use your professional summary from your CV.

Work Experience Section: A powerful one-line summary of your contributions at the job and your achievement-based bullet points from your CV.

Why? You want to accelerate opportunities to be invited for interviews directly from your profile.

Example:

Product Manager

Developing and launching strategic go-to-market initiatives for Product Teams

-Led release of new features, bringing in 200K+ subscriptions to the platform and £2M in revenue.

LinkedIn URL: Finally, update your LinkedIn URL to end in "/<firstname><lastname>"

Why? Lots of numbers and random letters in a URL do not look aesthetically pleasing. (Remember, you need your LinkedIn URL in your CV)

Applications: Your Action Plan

You have learnt about the 3 assets you need to prepare to get ready to start applying for jobs.

1. CV

2. Cover Letter

3. LinkedIn profile

Here's your action plan for the next 40 days of your job search (Day 11-50):

- Create versions of your CV tailored to job descriptions of interest
- Start drafting versions of Cover Letters for job descriptions
- Optimise your LinkedIn profile based on job descriptions
- Start applying to jobs (remember the 5 applications secret)

P.S. You can apply to more than 5 jobs but remember to be intentional and only apply to jobs you actually want!

CHAPTER 7:

INTERVIEWS

Mindset Shift: An application may get you an interview, but more is required to turn the interview into a job offer.

After applying for jobs, you will start getting invited to interview for roles.

In a nutshell, you secure the interview by looking good on paper (your applications).

However, you secure the job by bringing your work experience to life during the interview process.

At interviews, you need to be able to tell a compelling story about your career that positions you as the top candidate for the job you want. That is what gets you the job offer.

In this chapter, you are going to learn how to highlight your work experience and skills at interviews so you can secure the job.

Phone Interviews and Recruiter Conversations

Usually, when you are shortlisted for a job interview, you will be invited to an initial phone interview or to have a conversation with a recruiter.

This is an opportunity to articulate your experience in real life so they can see the person behind the application material (CV, Cover Letter, LinkedIn Profile). When you have gotten to this stage of the interview process, you must stick to your standards and start how you mean to continue. Do not settle for less when it comes to what you want out of your next job opportunity.

This initial phone interview or recruiter conversation is a good time to confirm that the job meets your requirements. E.g. Does it meet your salary expectations? Is it the seniority level you desire? This is so crucial. You want to avoid being disappointed later down the line so don't miss out on this early opportunity in the interview phase to re-validate that it suits your requirements.

Here is how to navigate when you are invited for a phone interview or to have a conversation with a recruiter:

First things first, celebrate! Your application was strong, and they are considering hiring you for the role but want to learn more about you first.

Even though they might call it a phone call or a "chat" with a recruiter, treat this conversation like you would a formal interview.

To start preparing make sure you do the following:

1. Have your salary expectations ready.

The "What are your salary expectations?" question will come up so it is important to be ready for it. If the question doesn't come up, you should ask, "What is the salary budgeted for this role?". Why? Because you do not want to move forward with an interview for a role that can't pay what you want.

2. Do research on the company and job position.

The recruiter will want to know why you want this job at this company. They will want to find out if you are a "serious candidate" and to know if you are really considering accepting the job offer should they give you an offer at the end of the interview process.

3. Practice introducing yourself

During the first conversation, to kick off the interview process, you'll need to know how to summarise your experience and highlight relevant experience regarding the role you've applied for. The recruiter already has your CV, so they want to have more context to find out if you are still a good fit for the job.

Questions to prepare answers to during the phone interview/recruiter conversation:

1. Introduce yourself/Walk me through your CV

The best way to answer this question is to talk about your professional experience so far and highlight the skills you have that are in the job description.

TIP: Have the job description and the CV you used to apply up on your screen if it's a phone/virtual interview

REMEMBER: The recruiter doesn't have first-hand knowledge of the role; they are only going off the job description so use this to your advantage!

2. Why this company?

Please research the company's recent news and read the news and blog section on their website.

Be honest with your answer but it's really important to show you are aware of the company's latest news and that you are aligned with their vision.

3. Why are you looking to move to this role/leave your current role?

Be as positive as possible and focus your answer on the job you applied for, not your current job. Never talk negatively about your employer (this comes off badly) or act like you are desperate to leave (you lose negotiation power later down the line).

Example of a good answer:

"I'm enjoying my current job but I'm always open to job opportunities that align with my future goals for my career.

This job is a perfect combination of what I would like to do next in my career: product launching, cross-functional team collaboration and marketing (insert relevant skills to the job here)."

4. What are your salary expectations?

No matter what you do, DO NOT share your current salary. Here is how to approach this question to ensure you share the salary you want for your next job (without restricting yourself to what you currently earn).

Approach 1: You have a clear walkaway number which is your minimum for any job

"I'm open to evaluating the entire compensation package for the role, including stocks and benefits but I am looking for an offer above (insert walkaway number) for my base salary."

Approach 2: You don't have enough data about the role budget and want to find out so you don't lowball yourself

"Thanks for asking (insert recruiter name), as you know more about the compensation at Company Name, it would be great to find out the salary range that has been budgeted for this role."

If the salary doesn't align with your expectations, ask if the budget is flexible. If it isn't, it's best to walk away before starting the interview process.

It's important to find out if your salary expectations will be met so you do not waste your time.

Interview Preparation

When you start interviewing for a new job, there might be several rounds of interviews. Typically, you should expect 1-3 rounds of interviews for junior to mid-level positions and anywhere between 4-6 rounds of interviews for senior/executive-level positions. Regardless of the level, your goal should be to show up as the top candidate by highlighting your relevant experience and competencies for the job. The secret to being the top candidate is: being confident and being competent.

If you step into the interviewer's shoes, the main questions they want to answer during the interview are:

- Is this a confident candidate? (a.k.a Are they personable/do I want to work with them?)

- Is this a competent candidate? (a.k.a Will they be able to do the job successfully?)

Your job is to make sure they feel the answer to the two questions above is a resounding "yes".

How to show confidence in interviews

- Your appearance: First impressions are important. No matter how laid back the company culture is, always dress smart and look put together (even if it is a virtual interview).

- Your speech: How you speak matters. Talking slowly helps you sound more eloquent and stops you from saying filler words.

- Your reasoning: People will form an opinion based on how you think. It's okay to pause so you can form well-thought-out and structured answers.

How to show competency in interviews

- How you answer interview questions: You will be asked about how you have dealt with certain scenarios in your career (More on this below).

- How you communicate your skills and experience: The most competent candidates have direct or transferable skills for the job. You will need to show how your past experience is relevant or complements the new job position you want.

Answering interview questions

During interviews, you will typically be asked competency questions to understand how you have navigated past scenarios in your career to see if you are a good fit for the job.

Examples:

- Tell me about a time you showed integrity and professionalism

- Tell me about a time you made a decision and then changed your mind

- Give an example of a time you handled conflict in the workplace

- Describe a situation in which you led a team

- Tell me about a time when your communication skills improved a situation

HINT: You'll be able to predict the type of competency questions you will be asked by reading the responsibilities listed in the job description.

To answer these types of questions, most people use a framework called STAR. However, I always suggest making a slight adjustment to this framework to make your answer more well-rounded

STARRY Framework

S=Situation

Give background on what point in your career you are speaking about

T=Task

Share your responsibility in that situation

A=Action

Explain your contribution regarding that task

R=Result

Talk about the outcome of your action

R=Reflect

Share what you learned and took away from the experience

Y=Why

Summarise everything you said and relate it back to the question you were asked

<u>Answering a competency question using the STARRY Framework</u>

Question: Tell me about a time you had to work with ambiguity and no guidance

S=Situation

When I was a marketing analyst at Monzo

T=Task

I worked on a project where I had to lead a marketing campaign for a brand-new feature for the application. It was a new feature that had never been created in the FinTech industry so I was pretty much starting from scratch.

A=Action

So, what I did was I went back to look into our past campaigns to see what went well and what didn't... Then I ran some tests to ensure I was gathering the right metrics... I drew up a marketing plan and worked with the ads team to...

R=Result

The result was we launched successfully and...

R=Reflect

What I learnt from this experience is that you can always get some direction from previous launches and...

Y=Why

In that role there were times when I had to handle ambiguity but doing effective market research helped me to deliver the best outcomes and I believe there will be situations in this job opportunity where I can successfully demonstrate this.

After The Interview

Right after the interview, you will often be asked if you have any questions.

You always need to have questions prepared!

Interviews are a two-way conversation. You might be more used to preparing to answer questions at interviews, but you also need to be prepared to ask questions as well. Companies interview you to find out if you're a good candidate, but you also need to find out if they are a good employer.

3 types of questions you should ask after an interview:

1. A question to help you get more context on what success looks like on the job

-Ask about responsibilities / team dynamics / company culture

E.g. What could I do in the first 3 months in the role to make an impact?

2. A question to understand your growth potential in the job and understand how performance is measured

   -Ask about career growth / professional development

   E.g. What are the opportunities for progression and promotion in the role and how often are performance reviews?

3. A question to be personable with the interviewer (people love to talk about themselves!)

   -Ask about the interviewer's experience in the role/at the company

   E.g. What's your experience on the team so far and what projects have you worked on?

So, now the interview is over. What should you do next?

To be a stand-out candidate, send a thank you email within 24 hours of the interview to the interviewers. If you don't have their contact details or have them as a connection on LinkedIn, send a thank you email to the recruiter.

Why? It could be a close call between you and other candidates in the hiring process. A thank you letter shows professionalism and enthusiasm and could solidify you as the top candidate.

Here are some templates you can use:

Template #1: Keeping it simple

Hi <**Interviewer Name**>,

It was so good to meet you today. Thanks for your consideration for the <**Job Title**> position. I'd love the opportunity to work with you and <**add impact you will make if you get the job here**.>

Best wishes,

<**Your name**>

Template #2: Revisiting the discussion

Hi <**Interviewer Name**>,

It was nice meeting with you today. It was great to learn more about your role at <**Company name**> and how you work with <**Something they mentioned**> to do <**Impact they mentioned**>. I could tell that a lot of great work has been done in the team so far and I'm excited about potentially working together and <**include some impact you would like to make when you join.**>

Many thanks

<**Your name**>

Interviews: Your Action Plan

You have learnt about the 3 key stages of the interview process and how you should prepare for them

1. Initial phone interview/recruiter conversation
2. The Main Interview process (1-3 interviews for junior/mid-level, 4-6 interviews for senior level)

3. After the interview: Questions for the interviewer and sending a thank you note

Here's your action plan for the next 30 days of your job search (Day 51-80):

Start preparing the following to get ready for your interviews.

- Review your CV ahead of the phone interview
- Prepare for your phone interview using these questions/prompts:

1. Introduce yourself/Walk me through your CV

2. Why this company?

3. Why are you looking to move to this role/leave your current role?

4. What are your salary expectations?

- Review the job description and the responsibilities shared in it.

- Use the STARRY Framework to prepare answers to potential questions (based on responsibilities in the job description)
- Prepare questions to ask the interviewer after the interview on the following topics:

1. Responsibilities/team dynamics/company culture

2. Career growth/professional development

3. The interviewer's experience in the role/at the company

CHAPTER 8:

JOB OFFERS & NEGOTIATION

Mindset Shift: The first offer is not the best offer.

Imagine this, you've implemented all of the previous 3 chapters (the first 3 phases of the Search To Secured Method) and you have started hearing back from companies you've interviewed with.

And it's good news! They want to hire you!

One of the best feelings in the world is being given a job offer for a job you are thrilled about. You've worked hard on your applications and preparing for interviews. However, there is still work to be done. Most people don't realise this and simply accept the first job offer that is presented to them.

This is a big mistake! The first job offer a company gives you is not always the best offer. You have to take your time selecting which job offer to go with and negotiate the best offer possible before you accept.

In this chapter, you will learn how to select the right job offer for you by negotiating so you can maximise your total compensation and perks at your new job.

Selecting The Job Offer

Before you decide to go with a job offer, you need to know what you can negotiate so you can maximise what you are offered as part of your package.

Most people think they can only negotiate their salary, but there is much more you can negotiate. This is extremely important when there is no further budget available to increase the salary offered. It's always good to know you can negotiate other things.

Here are the different parts of the offer you can negotiate:

1.   Base Salary

Most people tend to negotiate their salary alone.

REMEMBER:

When a job search is done right (by following the first 3 phases of the Search To Secured method), you'll be offered a salary that meets your expectations because before the interview, you asked for the budget or shared your salary expectations with the company.

By doing this, negotiating your salary is now an option, not a necessity.

2. Sign-On Bonus

A sign-on bonus is simply a bonus for signing your offer letter. This is usually a lump sum payment at the start of your employment. Many of my clients have been able to negotiate five-figure (£10k+) sign-on bonuses.

There are so many reasons for negotiating a sign-on bonus. Especially if you are leaving something behind if you stop working for your current employer. E.g. Quarterly/yearly bonus or stocks, or if you are moving cities or countries for the job and need some initial funds to facilitate your travel/initial accommodation.

3. Relocation Bonus

If you are moving cities or countries for the job, this is definitely something you should negotiate seeing as it requires you to relocate and resettle, which includes: travel, moving your items, accommodation, furniture etc.

4.   Professional Development/Training

If you have any professional development plans that will benefit the company if you pursue them, definitely negotiate this as part of your offer.

Name the qualification you are considering during your negotiation or ask for a budget to support your learning and growth.

5.   Reimbursements

Ask for a monthly allowance for something that will help you stay dedicated to doing your job well.

Will you be travelling as part of the job? Ask for a transport allowance.

Will you have to take calls with clients on the go? Ask for your phone bill to be covered.

Working late hours? Ask if there's a childcare discount for employees.

6.   Paid Vacation Days/ Work From Home Days

Negotiate for more days to make your work-life balance better.

Want to have more holidays in a year? Negotiate more paid vacation days.

Work better when you're remote? Negotiate fixed work-from-home days during the working week.

7.   Company Benefits/Perks

Do the benefits kick in later than your start day?

Share that a particular benefit (e.g. healthcare, pension, company stocks, fitness and wellness budget) is important to you and you need it to kick in by day 1 of your employment.

As you can see, negotiating your salary is important but there is much more you can negotiate beyond that.

Accepting The Job Offer

So many professionals find it difficult to navigate job offer conversations. They either say "Yes" to the job offer immediately or consider negotiating the job offer but chicken out because they are scared the company will take away the job offer if they try to negotiate.

Do not rush to accept a job offer. The company has taken their time and spent weeks reviewing your application and interviewing you, so they should also be ready for you to reflect on your decision before accepting their offer.

When you rush to immediately say "Yes", you lose your negotiating power because you have not taken time to review the offer and what is included.

Here is what most people do when they receive a job offer:

1. The company gives you a phone call or sends you an email offering you the job

2. You immediately accept the offer on the phone or via email

3. The company sends your offer letter

4. You sign the offer letter immediately

What this means for you is that you have no opportunity to negotiate your job offer and you lose out on maximising your job offer package.

Here is what you need to do moving forward when you receive a job offer:

1. The company gives you a phone call or sends you an email offering you the job

2. You express gratitude and ask for them to send the offer letter to you for you to review

3. The company sends your offer letter

4. You acknowledge the offer letter is received and ask for 2-5 working days to review the offer

5. You review the offer and prepare what you want to negotiate in the offer

6. You negotiate: This looks like scheduling a call/sending an email to the recruiter to adjust some items in the offer letter

7. Following negotiation, you review the offer letter again (or the updated offer letter if you mutually agreed on negotiated changes)

8. You sign the offer letter

In this scenario, you have more time to review what is included in the job offer, see how it benefits you and suggest some changes to be made. This gives you the best chance of making sure you accept a job offer that caters to you and your preferences.

Negotiation Preparation

When you have received your offer letter and asked for 2-5 working days to review it, there are 3 things you need to do to prepare to negotiate.

1. Do your research

- What is the salary budget for this type of job position? What does this company typically pay? Check pay transparency sites to find out this information.

- What do contacts in similar roles earn? Do you know anyone at the company or in a similar job position that can give you insight?

2.   Define your ideal offer

●   Does this job offer match or exceed the initial salary expectations you set at the beginning of the job search? If not, I suggest you start with negotiating salary first. If yes, start with negotiating bonuses and benefits (see the list of what you can negotiate in the selecting the job offer sub-section earlier on in this chapter).

3.   Decide on your most valuable skills and impact

●   A natural part of the negotiation conversation is pushback. Anticipate this! You really want to provide reasoning for why you want what you're asking for. I suggest you have at least three well-articulated points on your valuable skills and impact to use during the conversation. You can choose your most impressive achievement-based bullet points from your CV (that are relevant to this job position of course!).

Job Offers & Negotiation: Your Action Plan

You have learnt about the 3 parts to selecting, accepting and negotiating a job offer.

Here's your action plan for the next 10 days of your job search (Day 81-90):

- Thank the company for the offer and let them know that you will take 2-5 days to review the offer letter
- Decide what part of the job offer you want to negotiate
- Prepare for the negotiation conversation
- Negotiate: Schedule a call/send an email discussing your proposed changes to the offer letter
- Secure the job: Sign your offer letter and get ready to start your new job !

CHAPTER 9:

RESIGNING FROM YOUR JOB

Once you've accepted your job offer, most of the hard work is done. Now it's time to resign from your job. I always advise clients to make sure they have a job offer that has been signed and acknowledged by their future employer before they resign.

You never want to be in a situation where you resign from your job prematurely and have no job offer in hand.

The best way to resign from a job is to resign with grace. This means that you leave on a good note, without showing bad feelings or resentment towards your boss, colleagues or the organisation. It is likely that you are really excited to be leaving the company or have had some bad experiences that triggered you to start job searching in the first place but you still never want to come across badly when you resign.

In this chapter, I will share what you should consider before you resign, how to navigate your notice period and how to make a graceful transition from your old employer to your new job.

Things To Consider Before Resigning

1. Do I need to tell my employer where I am going? You don't have to share which company you are going to unless it's a competitor in the same industry. If it's a competitor, the right thing to do is disclose but be aware that most companies would want you to stop working immediately when you resign.

Many companies have trade secrets or special ways that they do things in their industry so they don't want you passing this information over to their competitors.

2. What should I do if I am moving to a company that is a competitor?

Check your employment contract to see if there's anything about gardening leave or a non-compete clause. When that exists, you might be asked to stop working immediately and not work for a competitor for up to a certain period so you do not share confidential information with your new employer.

I also recommend you seek professional legal advice to understand the implications of working with a competitor if there are any relevant clauses in your contract.

3.   What should I write in my resignation letter/email? Here is a handy template you can use:

Dear <Manager name>,

I would like to notify you that I am resigning from my position at <company name> effective immediately.

I will be serving my notice period of <number of weeks or months>, unless we jointly decide on a shorter period. In which case, I will be leaving the company earlier.

Thank you very much for the opportunity you've given me to contribute to the organisation and learn <skills and topics>. I am grateful for the opportunity and have enjoyed working with the team.

Yours sincerely,

<Your name>

4. How do I find out my notice period?

Your notice period is the duration of time you are expected to work at the company after you resign. When your notice period elapses, you will officially stop working and no longer be employed by the company.

Before you resign (a.k.a hand in your notice), find out what your notice period is from your employment contract. Your notice period may be negotiable, so feel free to discuss it with your manager.

Depending on the nature of the industry and job, some job positions have really long notice periods (3-4 months), but you can negotiate to something more reasonable, like 6-8 weeks, so you can start your new job sooner if you wish.

However, it is always safe to assume that the notice period in your employment contract is what's going to actually end up being used. So, it is reasonable to give your new employer a start date that is after the notice period for your current employer.

Making A Graceful Exit

As you start this new chapter of your career, it is important to leave your job with grace and not burn any bridges with any colleagues in your last few days on the job.

Here are some ways you can transition from your old job effectively:

1. Create effective handover documentation for your manager and colleagues so any projects you are working on can be passed on to another colleague.

2. Inform clients and important stakeholders that you'll be leaving once you've resigned just to ensure there's a flow of communication and expectations moving forward.

3. If it's part of your company culture, draft an email on your last working day thanking colleagues you have worked with during your time at the company.

Now it's time to move to greener pastures at your new job!

CHAPTER 10:

JOB SEARCH CONCERNS A.K.A "CAN I REALLY DO THIS?"

Since I developed the Search To Secured method, hundreds of women have used it to secure higher-paying and more fulfilling jobs. Before joining my coaching program, many of my clients had initial doubts about whether they could move jobs or thought their career situation was too complicated for them to leave the jobs they were currently in.

After joining the program, many of them were surprised at the confidence they built during their job search and the success of the method in helping them secure a new job opportunity.

In this chapter, I am going to go through the questions my clients had before using the Search To Secured Method to show you that if they can do it, you can do it too.

Situation #1: I want to get a job in [insert industry here], will it work for me?

Yes! Search To Secured is an adaptable job search strategy for securing a job in various industries. I have worked with women to move to higher-paying and more fulfilling roles in the following industries:

- Finance
- Marketing
- Technology
- Engineering
- Public Health
- Transport & Logistics
- Non-Profit
- Legal
- Oil & Gas
- Sustainable Development
- Government/Public Policy
- Healthcare
- Human Resources
- Education Administration
- Healthcare Administration
- Accounting
- Project/Program Management
- Operations

- Consulting

& so many other niche sectors

In my coaching program, I have worked with women to identify their transferrable skills and career achievements so they could stand out in the job market, be confident with their CV, Cover Letter and LinkedIn profile, breeze through the interview stage and secure job offers.

The Search To Secured Method has helped women secure management and leadership positions, break into a new industry and secure a pay rise without starting in a junior role.

If they could do it, you can do it too!

Situation #2: I need a remote job/a work visa sponsorship, will it work for me?

The Search To Secured method has helped dozens of women to obtain roles that fit their lifestyle or working requirement needs and you too can be one of them.

Clients inside my coaching program have been able to confidently identify companies and industries that would allow them to work remotely and sponsor their visas so they can work abroad. They have used the 4 phases of the method to also:

- Make their international experience relevant to the jobs they want and submit applications that stand out to recruiters and hiring managers.

- Convert their application into interviews and confidently prepare for interviews, answer competency questions and know the right questions to ask the interviewer.

- Receive high-paying job offers and negotiate additional perks such as a sign-on or relocation bonus to help them settle in as they move abroad.

If you want to work remotely or get a new job that moves you to another country, the Search To Secured Method can help you.

Situation #3: I want to move to a more senior position, will it work for me?

Yes! The Search To Secured method will help you articulate your achievements so you can secure a more senior position. Many of my clients have secured management and leadership roles without having official "manager" job titles before. Using this step-by-step process will show you exactly how to build a strong career story so you can secure jobs at the level you want.

I have helped my clients avoid wasting years thinking they were not qualified enough to get the jobs they wanted. Many of them were also considering going back to school to get Masters degrees. With the Search To Secured method, they have saved tens of thousands of pounds on education because they have been able to secure more senior jobs without going back to school.

Situation #4: I have many life commitments/I'm a busy mother and I need a new job that will help me have a better work-life balance, will it work for me?

Yes! Many of my clients have used the Search To Secured method to navigate the job market and get flexible jobs that allow them to work from home, at companies that promote well-being and work-life balance. I believe you shouldn't have to sacrifice your career to be present for your family. You can prioritise both.

The method is designed to work in 90 days or less! Many of my clients have secured new jobs while being business owners, postgraduate students, busy mothers and side hustlers. This program is designed to fit a busy woman's life. If it worked for them, it will work for you.

Situation #5: I know I am ready to move to a new job. I am worried about making mistakes during my job search or for it to take a long time, will it work for me?

Before working with me to use the Search To Secured method, many of my clients were thinking of or actively job searching for 6-12 months.

After working with me as their coach, they speed up their job search results and secure new roles anywhere between 3-12 weeks (less than 90 days!) and secure a new job giving them a £10k to £50k salary increase.

I intentionally designed this job search framework to eliminate the time and stress out of your job search. You will go from *overthinking and job searching for months* to peaceful and securing a new role within weeks.

Your Next Steps

1. Get inspired by other women's success stories

Check out success stories from my past clients who used the Search To Secured method. Check out my client results here https://coach-simi.com/client-results

2. Get support for your job search

Learn more about working with me. Check out my coaching program here https://coach-simi.com/search-to-secured

ACKNOWLEDGEMENTS

This book is a reflection of the love, dedication, and inspiration I've received throughout my journey supporting women in their careers. Countless people have made this project possible, and I'm filled with gratitude as I take a moment to acknowledge them.

First and foremost, I give all glory to God for His grace and unwavering presence throughout the process of writing this book. This journey has been one of faith, resilience, and trust in His divine timing, and I am beyond grateful for His blessings in every step of this process.

To Shanine, my publishing consultant, and Patrice, my editor, whose expertise, patience, and guidance helped shape this book into what it is today. Your belief in my vision and your commitment to excellence have been invaluable, and I am so grateful for your support throughout this process.

To my family and friends, you've been my anchors and my cheerleaders. Your encouragement has kept me grounded and motivated. Thank you for being there through every late night, every moment of self-doubt, and every victory, big and small. You are my constant source of strength.

To my darling children, thank you for showing me every day that it is possible to love deeply and be fully present in both motherhood and ambition. You are my greatest teachers, reminding me that we can create harmony between our dreams and our responsibilities. Your love fills my heart and fuels my purpose.

To my wonderful husband, words cannot fully express the depth of my gratitude. Your constant encouragement, belief in my abilities, and unwavering support have been the bedrock of my journey. Thank you for always seeing the best in me and standing by my side through it all.

And finally, to my incredible clients and every woman I have worked with in some shape or form, thank you for trusting me to be part of your career journey. It is a privilege I don't take lightly. Your courage to grow, evolve, and show up for yourselves in ways that challenge the status quo inspires me every day.

RESOURCES FOR YOUR JOB SEARCH

I am so excited to have played a part in your job search journey with this book. I never like to leave empty handed so here are some helpful resources for you!

Download your free 90-day job search plan

https://coach-simi.com/planner

Watch Job Search Training Videos:

3 types of career changes

https://youtu.be/GKRynamGRQU

How to find higher-paying jobs

https://youtu.be/1vnsJlmQjk0

Job Search Advice for mothers and mothers-to-be

https://youtu.be/Z3g-Jnl31sE

Sign up to receive emails with exclusive job search and career advice to help you secure a higher-paying and more fulfilling job

https://coach-simi.com/email

Check out success stories from my clients who secured new jobs using the Search To Secured Method

https://coach-simi.com/client-results

Learn more about working with me in my job search coaching program

https://coach-simi.com/search-to-secured

ABOUT THE AUTHOR

Simi Awokoya is an award-winning career coach, speaker, and the founder of the *Search To Secured* job search coaching program, designed specifically for Black women. After personally navigating the challenges of career transitions, Simi became passionate about helping women break through barriers so they never feel they have to settle. Through her coaching, workshops, and speaking engagements, Simi has empowered hundreds of women worldwide to increase their earning potential and transition into more fulfilling, rewarding careers.

Connect With Me

LinkedIn: Simi Awokoya

Instagram: @coachsimi

Website: https://coach-simi.com/

Email: hello@simiawokoya.com

www.ingramcontent.com/pod-product-compliance
Ingram Content Group UK Ltd.
Pitfield, Milton Keynes, MK11 3LW, UK
UKHW020215270125
454178UK00011B/580

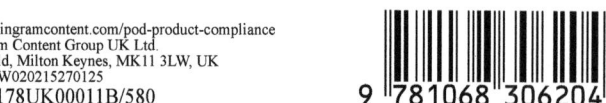